EASY LENTII COOKBOOK

50 EASY AND UNIQUE LENTIL RECIPES

3rd Edition

By
BookSumo Press
Copyright © by Saxonberg Associates

Published by
BookSumo Press, a DBA of Saxonberg Associates
http://www.booksumo.com/

ABOUT THE AUTHOR.

BookSumo Press is a publisher of unique, easy, and healthy cookbooks.

Our cookbooks span all topics and all subjects. If you want a deep dive into the possibilities of cooking with any type of ingredient. Then BookSumo Press is your go to place for robust yet simple and delicious cookbooks and recipes. Whether you are looking for great tasting pressure cooker recipes or authentic ethic and cultural food. BookSumo Press has a delicious and easy cookbook for you.

With simple ingredients, and even simpler step-by-step instructions BookSumo cookbooks get everyone in the kitchen chefing delicious meals.

BookSumo is an independent publisher of books operating in the beautiful Garden State (NJ) and our team of chefs and kitchen experts are here to teach, eat, and be merry!

INTRODUCTION

Welcome to *The Effortless Chef Series*! Thank you for taking the time to purchase this cookbook.

Come take a journey into the delights of easy cooking. The point of this cookbook and all BookSumo Press cookbooks is to exemplify the effortless nature of cooking simply.

In this book we focus on cooking with lentils. You will find that even though the recipes are simple, the taste of the dishes are quite amazing.

So will you take an adventure in simple cooking? If the answer is yes please consult the table of contents to find the dishes you are most interested in.

Once you are ready, jump right in and start cooking.

— BookSumo Press

TABLE OF CONTENTS

ANY ISSUES? CONTACT US

If you find that something important to you is missing from this book please contact us at info@booksumo.com.

We will take your concerns into consideration when the 2nd edition of this book is published. And we will keep you updated!

— BookSumo Press

LEGAL NOTES

COMMON ABBREVIATIONS

cup(s)	C.
tablespoon	tbsp
teaspoon	tsp
ounce	oz.
pound	lb

*All units used are standard American measurements

CHAPTER 1: EASY LENTIL RECIPES

LENTIL CURRY

Ingredients

- 2 C. red lentils
- 1 large onion, diced
- 1 tbsp vegetable oil
- 2 tbsps curry paste
- 1 tbsp curry powder
- 1 tsp ground turmeric
- 1 tsp ground cumin
- 1 tsp chili powder
- 1 tsp salt
- 1 tsp white sugar
- 1 tsp minced garlic
- 1 tsp minced fresh ginger
- 1 (14.25 oz.) can tomato puree

Directions

- Rinse your lentils and then put them in a saucepan submerged in fresh water.
- Get everything boiling and place a lid on the pot and cook it with a low level of heat for 22 mins.
- Now remove all the liquid.
- Get a bowl, combine until smooth: ginger, curry paste, garlic, curry powder, sugar, turmeric, salt, chili powder, and cumin.
- Stir fry your onions in veggie oil for 20 mins and pour in your spice mix.

- Continue stir frying for 2 more mins with a high heat level then add tomato puree and shut the heat.
- Combine the spicy onions with the lentils and stir everything until evenly coated.
- Enjoy.

Amount per serving (8 total)

Timing Information:

Preparation	Cooking	Total Time
10 m	30 m	40 m

Nutritional Information:

Calories	192 kcal
Fat	2.6 g
Carbohydrates	32.5g
Protein	12.1 g
Cholesterol	0 mg
Sodium	572 mg

* Percent Daily Values are based on a 2,000 calorie diet.

LENTILS FROM THE CARIBBEAN

Ingredients

- 1/4 C. canola oil
- 1 large onion, diced
- 2 carrots, peeled and diced
- salt and ground black pepper to taste
- 1/2 tsp white sugar
- 3 cloves garlic, minced
- 1 fresh chili pepper, minced
- 1 tsp grated fresh ginger
- 3 tbsps curry powder
- 2 (14 oz.) cans vegetable broth, divided
- 1 C. lentils
- 1/4 C. chopped fresh cilantro, or more to taste

Directions

- Cook your onions for 16 mins in a big pot in canola with the following: sugar, carrots, pepper, and salt. Then set the heat to low and combine in: curry, garlic, ginger, and chili peppers. Stir for 7 mins while heating.
- Turn up the heat on the stove and add 1 can of veggie broth and scrape the pot with a spoon.
- Pour in your lentils and the rest of the broth.
- Cook for 30 mins then add your cilantro.
- Enjoy.

Amount per serving (4 total)

Timing Information:

Preparation	Cooking	Total Time
25 m	50 m	1 h 15 m

Nutritional Information:

Calories	192 kcal
Fat	2.6 g
Carbohydrates	32.5g
Protein	12.1 g
Cholesterol	0 mg
Sodium	572 mg

* Percent Daily Values are based on a 2,000 calorie diet.

Lentil Soup I

(Red Lentils, Garlic, and Apricots)

Ingredients

- 3 tbsps olive oil
- 1 onion, chopped
- 2 cloves garlic, minced
- 1/3 C. dried apricots
- 1 1/2 C. red lentils
- 5 C. chicken stock
- 3 roma (plum) tomatoes - peeled, seeded and chopped
- 1/2 tsp ground cumin
- 1/2 tsp dried thyme
- salt to taste
- ground black pepper to taste
- 2 tbsps fresh lemon juice

Directions

- In olive oil stir fry your apricots, garlic, and onions for 2 mins. Then add in your stock and lentils and get everything boiling.
- Once boiling, lower the heat and let the contents cook for 30 mins.

- Add in the following after 30 mins: pepper, tomatoes, salt, cumin, and thyme.
- Cook for 12 more mins. Then combine in your lemon juice.
- Ladle out half of the soup and puree it in a blender then pour it back into the main mix.
- Enjoy warm.

Amount per serving (6 total)

Timing Information:

Preparation	Cooking	Total Time
15 m	50 m	1 h 5 m

Nutritional Information:

Calories	263 kcal
Fat	7.4 g
Carbohydrates	37.2g
Protein	13.2 g
Cholesterol	0 mg
Sodium	7 mg

* Percent Daily Values are based on a 2,000 calorie diet.

LENTIL SOUP II

(ONIONS, PARMESAN, AND WINE)

(HUNGARIAN STYLE LENTILS)

Ingredients

- 2 tbsps olive oil
- 2 large onions, cubed
- 1 tsp minced garlic
- 3 carrots, diced
- 2 stalks celery, diced
- 3 1/2 C. crushed tomatoes
- 1 1/2 C. lentils - soaked, rinsed and drained
- 1/2 tsp salt
- 1/2 tsp ground black pepper
- 3/4 C. white wine
- 2 bay leaves
- 7 C. chicken stock
- 1 sprig fresh parsley, chopped
- 1/2 tsp paprika
- 1/2 C. grated Parmesan cheese

Directions

- Stir fry your onions in a big pot until translucent then add in: carrots, garlic, celery, and paprika. Continue stir frying for 12 mins.
- Add in: pepper, tomatoes, salt, stock, bay leaves, and lentils. Mix the lentils a bit then pour in your wine and get the mixture boiling. Once everything is

boiling set the heat to low and let the mix simmer for 1 hr. Then add parmesan and parsley.

- Enjoy.

Amount per serving (8 total)

Timing Information:

Preparation	Cooking	Total Time
10 m	1 h 30 m	1 h 40 m

Nutritional Information:

Calories	255 kcal
Fat	6 g
Carbohydrates	33.3g
Protein	13.7 g
Cholesterol	9 mg
Sodium	1099 mg

* Percent Daily Values are based on a 2,000 calorie diet.

Mexican Style Lentils

Ingredients

- 1 tsp canola oil
- 2/3 C. finely chopped onion
- 1 small clove garlic, minced
- 2/3 C. dried lentils, rinsed
- 1 tbsp taco seasoning, or to taste
- 1 2/3 C. chicken broth
- 2/3 C. salsa
- 12 taco shells

Directions

- For 7 mins stir fry your onions in oil then add in your taco seasoning and stir everything before adding the lentils and cooking for 1 more min.
- Add your broth and get everything boiling.
- Once boiling, set the heat to low, and cook for 30 mins with a lid on the pot.
- Remove the lid and cook for 7 more mins to get it thicker then shut the heat and mash everything.
- Now add in the salsa and mix everything nicely.
- Divide the mix amongst your tacos and serve.
- Enjoy.

Amount per serving (6 total)

Timing Information:

Preparation	Cooking	Total Time
10 m	40 m	50 m

Nutritional Information:

Calories	304 kcal
Fat	10 g
Carbohydrates	44.2g
Protein	9.4 g
Cholesterol	1 mg
Sodium	714 mg

* Percent Daily Values are based on a 2,000 calorie diet.

Lentil Soup III

(Red Lentils, Sweet Potatoes, and Ginger)

Ingredients

- 1/4 C. butter
- 2 large sweet potatoes, peeled and chopped
- 3 large carrots, peeled and chopped
- 1 apple, peeled, cored and chopped
- 1 onion, chopped
- 1/2 C. red lentils
- 1/2 tsp minced fresh ginger
- 1/2 tsp ground black pepper
- 1 tsp salt
- 1/2 tsp ground cumin
- 1/2 tsp chili powder
- 1/2 tsp paprika
- 4 C. vegetable broth
- plain yogurt

Directions

- Stir fry the following in butter in a saucepan: onions, chunked sweet potatoes, apple, and carrots.
- Cook for 12 mins.
- Now add your veggie broth and the following: paprika, lentils, chili powder, ginger, cumin, black pepper, and salt.

- Get everything boiling, place a lid on the pot, and cook for 30 mins with a low heat.
- Puree the soup in batches and then add it to a separate pot or use an immersion blender to puree everything with one pot.
- Get the pureed soup boiling again and then lower the heat and cook for 12 more mins.
- Add a bit more water if the soup is too thick for your liking.
- When serving add a dollop of yogurt.
- Enjoy.

Amount per serving (6 total)

Timing Information:

Preparation	Cooking	Total Time
20 m	50 m	1 h 10 m

Nutritional Information:

Calories	322 kcal
Fat	9 g
Carbohydrates	52.9g
Protein	9 g
Cholesterol	22 mg
Sodium	876 mg

* Percent Daily Values are based on a 2,000 calorie diet.

LENTILS FROM ARABIA

Ingredients

- 1 C. dry lentils, rinsed
- 2 C. water
- 1 tsp salt
- 1 tbsp ground cumin
- 1 tbsp garlic powder
- 3/4 C. white rice, rinsed
- 3/4 C. water
- 1 tsp salt
- 2 tbsps olive oil
- 1/4 C. vegetable oil
- 3 white onions, sliced into 1/4-inch rings

Directions

- Boil, then simmer the following, with a low heat, for 25 mins, in a big pot: garlic powder, 2 C. of water, cumin, and salt (1 tsp).
- Now add in: olive oil, rice, salt (1 tsp), and 3/4 C. of water.
- Put a lid on the pot and cook for 40 mins with a low heat until the rice is soft.
- Simultaneously stir fry your onions in oil for 12 mins then top the lentils with the onions when everything is finished cooking.
- Enjoy.

Amount per serving (6 total)

Timing Information:

Preparation	Cooking	Total Time
15 m	1 h 10 m	1 h 25 m

Nutritional Information:

Calories	371 kcal
Fat	14.4 g
Carbohydrates	49.8g
Protein	11.6 g
Cholesterol	0 mg
Sodium	788 mg

* Percent Daily Values are based on a 2,000 calorie diet.

LENTILS FROM THE MEDITERRANEAN

Ingredients

- 1 tbsp olive oil
- 1 1/2 lbs lamb shoulder arm chops, cubed, round bones reserved
- 1 tsp salt
- 1/2 tsp ground black pepper
- 1 onion, chopped
- 4 cloves garlic, minced
- 1 C. lentils, picked over and rinsed
- 2 C. chicken broth, or more as needed
- 1 (14 oz.) can diced tomatoes
- 3 carrots, peeled and sliced
- 1/2 tsp dried thyme
- 1/2 tsp dried sage
- 1/2 tsp dried basil
- 2 C. coarsely chopped fresh spinach
- 1 lemon, juiced and zested
- 1/2 C. ricotta cheese, crumbled

Directions

- Stir fry your lamb for 3 mins until browned, in hot oil, then add pepper and salt.
- Cook this mix for 1 more min.
- Now combine in: garlic and onions.
- Cook for 2 more mins while stirring.

- Add the following: basil, lentils, sage, 2 C. broth, thyme, tomatoes, and carrots.
- Get everything boiling and then place a lid on the pot and let the contents lightly boil for 25 mins.
- Add a C. more of broth if necessary then take out the bones from the lamb and add in the spinach and cook for 7 more mins before adding the lemon juice and zest.
- When serving top with cheese.
- Enjoy.

Amount per serving (4 total)

Timing Information:

Preparation	Cooking	Total Time
15 m	40 m	55 m

Nutritional Information:

Calories	572 kcal
Fat	26.7 g
Carbohydrates	46.4g
Protein	39.3 g
Cholesterol	103 mg
Sodium	1049 mg

* Percent Daily Values are based on a 2,000 calorie diet.

Lentil Soup IV

(Red Lentils, Coconut, and Tomatoes)

(Vegan Approved)

Ingredients

- 1 tbsp peanut oil
- 1 small onion, chopped
- 1 tbsp minced fresh ginger root
- 1 clove garlic, chopped
- 1 pinch fenugreek seeds
- 1 C. dry red lentils
- 1 C. butternut squash - peeled, seeded, and cubed
- 1/3 C. finely chopped fresh cilantro
- 2 C. water
- 1/2 (14 oz.) can coconut milk
- 2 tbsps tomato paste
- 1 tsp curry powder
- 1 pinch cayenne pepper
- 1 pinch ground nutmeg
- salt and pepper to taste

Directions

- Stir fry, until soft: fenugreek, onions, garlic, and ginger. Then add in: tomato paste, pepper, curry powder, cilantro, salt, water, lentils, cayenne, coconut milk, nutmeg, and squash.

- Get everything boiling and cook for 32 mins.
- Enjoy.

Amount per serving (4 total)

Timing Information:

Preparation	Cooking	Total Time
15 m	40 m	55 m

Nutritional Information:

Calories	303 kcal
Fat	14.6 g
Carbohydrates	34.2g
Protein	13 g
Cholesterol	0 mg
Sodium	81 mg

* Percent Daily Values are based on a 2,000 calorie diet.

HEARTY HAM AND LENTILS

Ingredients

- 1 C. dried lentils
- 1 C. chopped celery
- 1 C. chopped carrots
- 1 C. chopped onion
- 2 cloves garlic, minced
- 1 1/2 C. diced cooked ham
- 1/2 tsp dried basil
- 1/4 tsp dried thyme
- 1/2 tsp dried oregano
- 1 bay leaf
- 1/4 tsp black pepper
- 32 oz. chicken broth
- 1 C. water
- 8 tsps tomato sauce

Directions

- Add the following to your crock pot: pepper, lentils, bay leaf, celery, oregano, carrots, thyme, onions, basil, ham, and garlic. Pour in the broth and place a lid on the slow cooker. Let the contents cook on low for 12 hours.
- Enjoy.

Amount per serving (6 total)

Timing Information:

Preparation	Cooking	Total Time
20 m	12 h	12 h 20 m

Nutritional Information:

Calories	222 kcal
Fat	6.1 g
Carbohydrates	26.3g
Protein	15.1 g
Cholesterol	20 mg
Sodium	1170 mg

* Percent Daily Values are based on a 2,000 calorie diet.

LENTILS FROM MOROCCO

Ingredients

- 2 onions, chopped
- 2 cloves garlic, minced
- 1 tsp grated fresh ginger
- 6 C. water
- 1 C. red lentils
- 1 (15 oz.) can garbanzo beans, drained
- 1 (19 oz.) can cannellini beans
- 1 (14.5 oz.) can diced tomatoes
- 1/2 C. diced carrots
- 1/2 C. chopped celery
- 1 tsp garam masala
- 1 1/2 tsps ground cardamom
- 1/2 tsp ground cayenne pepper
- 1/2 tsp ground cumin
- 1 tbsp olive oil

Directions

- Stir fry the following, in a saucepan, in olive oil, for 7 mins: ginger, garlic, and onions.

- Pour in your water, cumin, lentils, cayenne, chick peas, cardamom, kidney beans, masala, tomatoes, celery, and carrots.
- Get the mix boiling, then lower the heat for a gentle simmer for 2 hrs.
- Puree about one half of the soup in a blender and then mix it back into the saucepan before serving.
- Enjoy.

Amount per serving (6 total)

Timing Information:

Preparation	Cooking	Total Time
20 m	1 h 45 m	2 h 5 m

Nutritional Information:

Calories	329 kcal
Fat	3.6 g
Carbohydrates	56.5g
Protein	18.3 g
Cholesterol	0 mg
Sodium	317 mg

* Percent Daily Values are based on a 2,000 calorie diet.

Easy Sausage and Lentils

Ingredients

- 1 (16 oz.) package dry lentils
- 1 (16 oz.) can diced tomatoes, drained
- 2 (14 oz.) cans beef broth
- 3 C. water
- 1 carrot, chopped
- 2 lbs kielbasa (Polish) sausage, cut into 1/2 inch pieces
- 1 stalk celery, chopped

Directions

- Run some fresh water over your lentils then place them in a crock pot with: celery, tomatoes, sausage, broth, carrots, and water.
- Place a lid on the slow cooker and let the contents cook for 3 hours on high or 8 hours on low. Stir then serve.
- Enjoy.

Amount per serving (12 total)

Timing Information:

Preparation	Cooking	Total Time
15 m	3 h	3 h 15 m

Nutritional Information:

Calories	357 kcal
Fat	21.2 g
Carbohydrates	22.8g
Protein	18.8 g
Cholesterol	50 mg
Sodium	966 mg

* Percent Daily Values are based on a 2,000 calorie diet.

Artisan Style Shiitake Mushrooms and Lentils

Ingredients

- 2 quarts vegetable broth
- 2 C. sliced fresh button mushrooms
- 1 oz. dried shiitake mushrooms, torn into pieces
- 3/4 C. uncooked pearl barley
- 3/4 C. dry lentils
- 1/4 C. dried onion flakes
- 2 tsps minced garlic
- 2 tsps dried summer savory
- 3 bay leaves
- 1 tsp dried basil
- 2 tsps ground black pepper
- salt to taste

Directions

- Add the following to a crock pot: salt, broth, pepper, mushrooms, basil, barley, bay leaves, lentils, savory, onion flakes, and garlic. Place a lid on the slow cook and cook for 6 hrs on high or 12 hrs on low.
- Enjoy.

Amount per serving (8 total)

Timing Information:

Preparation	Cooking	Total Time
15 m	12 h	12 h 15 m

Nutritional Information:

Calories	213 kcal
Fat	1.2 g
Carbohydrates	43.9g
Protein	8.4 g
Cholesterol	0 mg
Sodium	466 mg

* Percent Daily Values are based on a 2,000 calorie diet.

RUSTIC LENTILS WITH SAVORY CHICKEN

Ingredients

- 1 tbsp olive oil
- 2 lbs bone-in chicken pieces
- 1 large onion, finely chopped
- 1 small carrot, finely chopped
- 2 cloves garlic, finely chopped
- 3/4 C. dried lentils
- 1 (14 oz.) can chicken broth
- 1/2 tsp salt
- 1 (10 oz.) can tomato sauce
- 1/2 tsp dried rosemary
- 1/2 tsp dried basil
- 1 tbsp lemon juice

Directions

- Stir fry your chicken, in oil, in a big pot for 6 mins per side and then place the chicken to the side.
- Now stir fry your onions for 6 mins in the same pan and then add in the garlic, lentils, salt, broth, and carrots.

- Get everything boiling and then place a lid on the pot and cook for 22 mins over low heat.
- Now add back in, your chicken, and let the contents keep simmering for 20 more mins with a lid on the pot.
- Add water if needed then add in your tomato sauce, basil, and rosemary.
- Let the tomato sauce cook for 10 mins and finally combine in the lemon juice.
- Enjoy.

Amount per serving (6 total)

Timing Information:

Preparation	Cooking	Total Time
15 m	1 h 15 m	1 h 30 m

Nutritional Information:

Calories	308 kcal
Fat	13.5 g
Carbohydrates	18.7g
Protein	27.8 g
Cholesterol	68 mg
Sodium	816 mg

* Percent Daily Values are based on a 2,000 calorie diet.

Lentil Soup V

(Jalapenos, Black Beans, and Peppers)

Ingredients

- 1 lb dry black beans
- 1 1/2 quarts water
- 1 carrot, chopped
- 1 stalk celery, chopped
- 1 large red onion, chopped
- 6 cloves garlic, crushed
- 2 green bell peppers, chopped
- 2 jalapeno pepper, seeded and minced
- 1/4 C. dry lentils
- 1 (28 oz.) can peeled and diced tomatoes
- 2 tbsps chili powder
- 2 tsps ground cumin
- 1/2 tsp dried oregano
- 1/2 tsp ground black pepper
- 3 tbsps red wine vinegar
- 1 tbsp salt
- 1/2 C. uncooked white rice

Directions

- Submerge your beans in about 3 times their size of water.
- Then get everything boiling for 12 mins.
- Now place a lid on the pan and shut the heat.
- Let the beans sit for 1 and a half hours before removing the liquid and then rinsing the beans.

- Add your beans to a slow cooker with 1.5 quarts of fresh water and cook for 3 hrs on high.
- Now add the following after 3 hrs of cooking: tomatoes, carrots, lentils, celery, salt, chili powder, vinegar, cumin, black pepper, and oregano, jalapenos, onions, bell peppers, and garlic.
- With low heat cook for 3 more hrs. Then add the rice when about 25 mins is left in the cooking time.
- Take half of the soup and puree it in a blender then put it back in the pot.
- Enjoy.

Amount per serving (10 total)

Timing Information:

Preparation	Cooking	Total Time
1 h	5 h	6 h

Nutritional Information:

Calories	231 kcal
Fat	1.2 g
Carbohydrates	43.4g
Protein	12.6 g
Cholesterol	0 mg
Sodium	851 mg

* Percent Daily Values are based on a 2,000 calorie diet.

Artisan Lentil Bake

Ingredients

- 1 1/8 C. green lentils
- 2 1/4 C. water
- 6 slices white bread, torn into small pieces
- 2 eggs
- 1 C. vegetable broth
- 2 tbsps tomato paste
- 1/2 tsp dried basil
- 1/4 tsp garlic powder
- 1/2 tsp ground black pepper
- 1 tsp dried parsley
- 1 tbsp olive oil
- 1/2 packet dry vegetable soup mix
- 1/3 C. dried bread crumbs

Directions

- Boil your lentils and water for 3 mins then set the heat to low and let everything gently boil for 40 mins.
- Oil a bread pan and then set your oven to 400 degrees before doing anything else.

- Get a bowl, combine: soup mix, 2 C. of cooked lentils, olive oil, bread, parsley, eggs, black pepper, broth, garlic powder, tomato paste, and basil. Then enter everything into a bread pan.
- Cook the loaf in the oven for 40 mins. Then top with bread crumps and cook for 12 more mins. Let the contents cool for 15 mins before cutting.
- Enjoy.

Amount per serving (6 total)

Timing Information:

Preparation	Cooking	Total Time
45 m	50 m	1 h 35 m

Nutritional Information:

Calories	272 kcal
Fat	5.6 g
Carbohydrates	40.9g
Protein	14.6 g
Cholesterol	62 mg
Sodium	369 mg

* Percent Daily Values are based on a 2,000 calorie diet.

GREEK INSPIRED SALAD OF LENTILS

Ingredients

- 1 C. dry brown lentils
- 1 C. diced carrots
- 1 C. red onion, diced
- 2 cloves garlic, minced
- 1 bay leaf
- 1/2 tsp dried thyme

- 2 tbsps lemon juice
- 1/2 C. diced celery
- 1/4 C. chopped parsley
- 1 tsp salt
- 1/4 tsp ground black pepper
- 1/4 C. olive oil

Directions

- Get a big pot add in: thyme, lentils, bay leaves, carrots, garlic, and onions.
- Submerge everything in water then get it all boiling, set the heat to low, and cook for 22 mins with a light boil.
- Now remove all the liquid and the bay leaf.
- Pour in your olive oil, pepper, lemon juice, salt, celery, and parsley.
- Stir to evenly coat and serve when it has completely cooled off.
- Enjoy.

Amount per serving (8 total)

Timing Information:

Preparation	Cooking	Total Time
10 m	20 m	30 m

Nutritional Information:

Calories	147 kcal
Fat	7.1 g
Carbohydrates	16.2g
Protein	6 g
Cholesterol	0 mg
Sodium	453 mg

* Percent Daily Values are based on a 2,000 calorie diet.

SOUTH AMERICAN STYLE LENTILS

(PEAS, APPLES, AND TOMATOES)

Ingredients

- 1 C. dry lentils
- 1 quart water
- 1 cube vegetable bouillon
- 3 medium tomatoes, peeled and diced
- 1 large onion, diced
- 1 carrot, sliced
- 1 medium apple - peeled, cored and diced
- 1/2 C. frozen peas
- 1 large clove garlic
- 1 tbsp olive oil
- 1/4 C. barbeque sauce
- 1/2 tsp paprika
- salt and pepper to taste

Directions

- Boil the following, then simmer it over low heat, for 22 mins: water, veggie bouillon, and lentils.
- After 22 mins add in: paprika, tomatoes, bbq sauce, onions, olive oil, carrots, garlic, apple, and peas. Cook for 22 more mins.
- Then add your preferred amount of pepper and salt.
- Enjoy.

Amount per serving (4 total)

Timing Information:

Preparation	Cooking	Total Time
15 m	40 m	55 m

Nutritional Information:

Calories	266 kcal
Fat	4.3 g
Carbohydrates	46.3g
Protein	13.4 g
Cholesterol	0 mg
Sodium	225 mg

* Percent Daily Values are based on a 2,000 calorie diet.

Easy Ditalini Pasta

Ingredients

- 1 onion, chopped
- 3 cloves garlic, minced
- 2 tbsps olive oil
- 1 (19 oz.) can lentil soup
- 1 C. crushed tomatoes
- 1 (10 oz.) package frozen chopped spinach
- 1 (16 oz.) package ditalini pasta
- salt to taste
- ground black pepper to taste
- 1 pinch crushed red pepper
- 2 tbsps grated Parmesan cheese

Directions

- Fry your garlic and onions until browned and then add in your tomatoes and lentils. Get the mix boiling and add the spices and spinach.
- Simultaneously boil your pasta in water and salt for 9 mins. Then remove all the liquid. Now add it to the lentils. Place a lid on everything and cook it all over a very high heat for 22 mins.
- Enjoy.

Amount per serving (6 total)

Timing Information:

Preparation	Cooking	Total Time
15 m	30 m	45 m

Nutritional Information:

Calories	407 kcal
Fat	7.1 g
Carbohydrates	70.5g
Protein	15.9 g
Cholesterol	1 mg
Sodium	282 mg

* Percent Daily Values are based on a 2,000 calorie diet.

PORTUGUESE INSPIRED LENTILS

Ingredients

- 1 tbsp olive oil
- 2 cloves garlic, sliced
- 3/4 lb bulk chorizo sausage
- 5 ribs celery, sliced
- 1 C. dried lentils
- 3 C. water
- 1 tsp ground dried turmeric
- 1 tsp curry powder
- 1 tsp ground cumin
- salt and pepper to taste

Directions

- Stir fry your garlic for 1 min in olive oil in a big pot then add in your sausage and fry for 5 mins.
- Now add the celery and cook for 5 more mins continuing to stir and fry. Now combine in the water, cumin, curry, turmeric and lentils.
- Get everything boiling then place a lid on the pot and set the heat to low and let the contents gently boil for 40 mins.
- Add your preferred amount of pepper and salt and then serve.
- Enjoy.

Amount per serving (4 total)

Timing Information:

Preparation	Cooking	Total Time
10 m	50 m	1 h

Nutritional Information:

Calories	611 kcal
Fat	36.9 g
Carbohydrates	34.9g
Protein	33.9 g
Cholesterol	75 mg
Sodium	1145 mg

* Percent Daily Values are based on a 2,000 calorie diet.

Coconut Quinoa

Ingredients

- 2 C. quinoa
- 3 1/2 C. water
- 1 tbsp salt
- 2 tbsps coconut oil
- 1 small onion, chopped
- 6 cloves garlic, minced
- 5 large tomatoes, chopped
- 1 C. water
- 1 (14 oz.) can coconut milk
- 1 tbsp molasses
- 1/4 C. coconut powder
- 1 (4 inch) cinnamon stick
- 3 tbsps curry powder
- 2 tbsps ground coriander
- 2 C. red lentils
- salt and pepper to taste
- 1 bunch fresh cilantro, chopped

Directions

- Submerge your quinoa in water, in a bowl, for 10 mins. Then remove all the liquid and run the quinoa under fresh cold water.
- Now boil the quinoa in 3.5 C. of water and 1 tsp of salt for 17 mins.
- Place a lid on the pan and cook with a lower level of heat.
- Stir fry your garlic and onions in coconut oil for 7 mins. Then add in the coconut milk and the water, coriander, molasses, curry powder, coconut powder, and cinnamon.
- Get everything boiling and then add the lentils and cook for 15 mins with a low level of heat.

- Make sure to stir every 3 to 5 mins.
- Now add your preferred amount of pepper and salt. Top with cilantro.
- Layer the lentils over the quinoa.
- Enjoy.

Amount per serving (12 total)

Timing Information:

Preparation	Cooking	Total Time
25 m	35 m	1 h

Nutritional Information:

Calories	347 kcal
Fat	13.5 g
Carbohydrates	45.5g
Protein	14.4 g
Cholesterol	0 mg
Sodium	602 mg

* Percent Daily Values are based on a 2,000 calorie diet.

Lentils from Germany

Ingredients

- 2 C. dried brown lentils, rinsed and drained
- 3 C. chicken stock
- 1 bay leaf
- 1 C. chopped carrots
- 1 C. chopped celery
- 1 C. chopped onion
- 1 C. cooked, cubed ham
- 1 tsp Worcestershire sauce
- 1/2 tsp garlic powder
- 1/4 tsp freshly grated nutmeg
- 5 drops hot pepper sauce
- 1/4 tsp caraway seed
- 1/2 tsp celery salt
- 1 tbsp chopped fresh parsley
- 1/2 tsp ground black pepper

Directions

- Add the following to a crock pot: ham, lentils, pepper, Worcestershire, parsley, garlic powder, celery salt, nutmeg, caraway, hot sauce, onions, stock, carrots, and bay leaf.
- Place a lid on the slow cooker and let go for 9 hrs on low.
- Enjoy over cooked rice.

Amount per serving (8 total)

Timing Information:

Preparation	Cooking	Total Time
10 m	8 h	8 h 10 m

Nutritional Information:

Calories	221 kcal
Fat	2.3 g
Carbohydrates	34.2g
Protein	16 g
Cholesterol	10 mg
Sodium	608 mg

* Percent Daily Values are based on a 2,000 calorie diet.

Easy Dahl

Ingredients

- 1 C. red lentils
- 2 tbsps ginger root, minced
- 1 tsp mustard seed
- 2 tbsps chopped fresh cilantro
- 4 tomatoes, chopped
- 3 onions, chopped
- 3 jalapeno peppers, seeded and minced
- 1 tbsp ground cumin
- 1 tbsp ground coriander seed
- 6 cloves garlic, minced
- 2 tbsps olive oil
- 1 C. water
- salt to taste

Directions

- Pressure cook the lentils until tender or boil them in water for 22 mins.
- Stir fry your mustard seeds until they being to pop then add in your oil, garlic, onions, jalapenos, and ginger.
- Continue stirring and frying until the onions are browned.

- Now pour in your tomatoes, cumin, and coriander.
- Cook the tomatoes for 2 mins and then add in your water and boil everything for 7 mins.
- Combine in your cooked lentils and mix everything.
- Finally add your preferred amount of salt.
- Serve with cilantro.
- Enjoy with cooked basmati.

Amount per serving (6 total)

Timing Information:

Preparation	Cooking	Total Time
10 m	40 m	50 m

Nutritional Information:

Calories	209 kcal
Fat	5.7 g
Carbohydrates	30.6g
Protein	10.4 g
Cholesterol	0 mg
Sodium	12 mg

* Percent Daily Values are based on a 2,000 calorie diet.

SAVORY POTATOES AND LENTILS

Ingredients

- 2 C. vegetable broth, divided
- 1 tsp yeast extract spread, e.g. Marmite/Vegemite
- 1/2 C. dry lentils
- 1/4 C. pearl barley
- 1 large carrot, diced
- 1/2 onion, finely chopped
- 1/2 C. walnuts, coarsely chopped
- 3 potatoes, chopped
- 1 tsp all-purpose flour
- 1/2 tsp water
- salt and pepper to taste

Directions

- Set your oven to 350 degrees before doing anything else.
- For 32 mins lightly boil: barley, 1.25 C. of broth, lentils, and yeast.
- Simultaneously simmer for 17 mins: walnuts, the rest of the broth, onions, and carrots. After the 17 mins is done add in your flour and water.
- Also at the same time boil your potatoes in water and salt for 17 mins. Then remove the liquid and mash them.

- Mix the carrots with the lentils.
- Add some pepper and salt and combine everything in a baking dish and top with the potatoes.
- Cook the contents in the oven for 32 mins.
- Enjoy.

Amount per serving (8 total)

Timing Information:

Preparation	Cooking	Total Time
15 m	1 h	1 h 15 m

Nutritional Information:

Calories	184 kcal
Fat	5.2 g
Carbohydrates	29.8g
Protein	6.2 g
Cholesterol	0 mg
Sodium	147 mg

* Percent Daily Values are based on a 2,000 calorie diet.

LENTILS AND CHARD WITH MUSHROOMS

Ingredients

- 1 tbsp olive oil
- 1 onion, diced
- 3 cloves garlic, minced
- 2 C. uncooked quinoa, rinsed
- 1 C. canned lentils, rinsed
- 8 oz. fresh mushrooms, chopped
- 1 quart vegetable broth
- 1 bunch Swiss chard, stems removed

Directions

- Stir fry your onions and garlic in a saucepan in oil for 7 mins. Add in the mushrooms, lentils, broth and quinoa.
- Get everything boiling and then place a lid on the pot and cook the contents with a lower level of heat for 20 mins.
- Shut the heat and add in your chards then stir to distribute them evenly.
- Place the lid back on the pot and let them sit for 7 mins.
- Enjoy.

Amount per serving (8 total)

Timing Information:

Preparation	Cooking	Total Time
20 m	20 m	40 m

Nutritional Information:

Calories	224 kcal
Fat	4.7 g
Carbohydrates	36.6g
Protein	9.6 g
Cholesterol	0 mg
Sodium	323 mg

* Percent Daily Values are based on a 2,000 calorie diet.

Italian Style Lentils with Zucchini

Ingredients

- 2 tsps olive oil
- 1 C. chopped onion
- 2 C. fresh sliced mushrooms
- 1 small zucchini, chopped
- 3 cloves garlic, minced
- 1 C. dry lentils
- 3 C. water
- 2 (8 oz.) cans tomato sauce
- 1 (6 oz.) can tomato paste
- 1 1/2 tsps white sugar
- 1/2 C. water

Directions

- Stir fry, for 7 mins: garlic, onions, zucchini, and mushrooms. Then add in lentils and water (3 C.).
- Get everything boiling then lower the heat to a gentle boil and place a lid on the pot.
- Let everything cook for 40 mins.
- Now add in your tomato sauce and paste, half a C. of water, and your sugar.

- Get it all boiling again, lower the heat to low, and place a lid on the pot.
- Cook for 23 more mins and everything should be nice and thick.
- Enjoy with pasta.

Amount per serving (8 total)

Timing Information:

Preparation	Cooking	Total Time
20 m	1 h 20 m	1 h 40 m

Nutritional Information:

Calories	145 kcal
Fat	1.8 g
Carbohydrates	25.5g
Protein	8.9 g
Cholesterol	0 mg
Sodium	466 mg

* Percent Daily Values are based on a 2,000 calorie diet.

INDIAN STYLE POTATOES AND LENTILS

Ingredients
- 3 tbsps vegetable oil
- 1 1/2 pounds potatoes, cut into 1/2 inch dice
- 2 1/2 C. cauliflower florets
- 1 large onion, sliced
- 2 cloves garlic, crushed
- 1 tbsp curry powder
- 1/2 tbsp ground ginger
- 4 oz. dry red lentils
- 1 (14.4 oz.) can whole tomatoes, diced
- 1 1/4 C. vegetable stock
- 2 tbsps malt vinegar
- 1 tbsp mango chutney
- salt and pepper to taste
- diced fresh parsley for garnish

Directions
- Stir fry the following in oil until brown: potatoes, garlic, cauliflower, and onion.
- Add the ginger and curry and cook for 5 more mins.
- Now add: chutney, lentils, vinegar, stock, and tomatoes.
- Top everything with some pepper and salt and cook the mix with a lid on the pot for 22 mins.
- When serving add some parsley.
- Enjoy.

Amount per serving (4 total)

Timing Information:

Preparation	Cooking	Total Time
30 m	30 m	1 h

Nutritional Information:

Calories	395 kcal
Fat	11.4 g
Carbohydrates	62.9g
Protein	14 g
Cholesterol	0 mg
Sodium	272 mg

* Percent Daily Values are based on a 2,000 calorie diet.

BLACKENED CHAMPAGNE LENTILS

Ingredients
- 1 tbsp butter
- 1 tbsp olive oil
- 1/2 C. diced onion
- 1/2 C. diced carrot
- 1/2 C. diced celery
- salt to taste
- 6 sprigs fresh thyme
- ground black pepper to taste
- 1 C. beluga lentils
- 1 3/4 C. chicken stock
- 1 tbsp champagne vinegar
- 2 tbsps diced Italian parsley

Directions
- Stir fry the following in olive oil and butter: salt, onions, celery, and carrots.
- Let the mix cook for 12 mins.
- Now set the heat to low and combine in: pepper and thyme sprigs.
- Add the lentils and stir the contents then pour in the stock and get everything boiling with a high heat.
- Once the mix is boiling, place a lid on the pot, set the heat to low again, and cook the lentils for 37 mins.

- Remove the pieces of thyme and add the vinegar, more salt, pepper, and also some parsley.
- Enjoy.

Amount per serving (2 total)

Timing Information:

Preparation	Cooking	Total Time
15 m	45 m	1 h

Nutritional Information:

Calories	500 kcal
Fat	14.3 g
Carbohydrates	68g
Protein	26.6 g
Cholesterol	16 mg
Sodium	698 mg

* Percent Daily Values are based on a 2,000 calorie diet.

Lentil Salad I

Ingredients
- 2 C. lentil sprouts
- 1/2 C. seeded, diced cucumber
- 1/2 C. seeded, diced tomato
- 1/3 C. diced green onions
- 2 tbsps diced fresh cilantro
- 1/2 C. thinly sliced radishes (optional)
- 1 tbsp olive oil
- 2 tbsps lemon juice
- 1 tbsp white wine vinegar
- 1 1/2 tsps dried oregano
- 1/2 tsp garlic powder
- 1 1/2 tsps curry powder
- 1/2 tsp dry mustard
- 1 pinch salt and pepper to taste

Directions
- Get a bowl, mix: radish, lentil sprouts, cilantro, cucumber, green onions, and tomatoes.
- Get 2nd bowl, combine: pepper, olive oil, salt, lemon juice, mustard, vinegar, curry, and oregano.
- Now combine both bowls and place the contents in the fridge for 40 mins to get cold with a covering of plastic around the bowl.
- Enjoy.

Amount per serving (8 total)

Timing Information:

Preparation	Cooking	Total Time
15 m		35 m

Nutritional Information:

Calories	46 kcal
Fat	2 g
Carbohydrates	6.5g
Protein	2.2 g
Cholesterol	0 mg
Sodium	56 mg

* Percent Daily Values are based on a 2,000 calorie diet.

Easy Pepper and Tomato Lentils

Ingredients
- 1 quart water
- 1 C. dry lentils
- 3 tbsps olive oil
- 1 medium green bell pepper, diced
- 1 medium onion, diced
- 2 1/2 C. peeled, seeded, and diced tomatoes
- salt and pepper to taste

Directions
- Get your lentils boiling in water, set the heat to low, and let the contents cook for 22 mins. Then remove any leftover liquids.
- Now begin to stir fry your onions and bell peppers in olive oil until the onion is soft then add pepper, salt, and the tomatoes.
- Combine in the lentils as well and let the contents cook for 32 mins with a low heat and no cover.
- Enjoy.

Amount per serving (4 total)

Timing Information:

Preparation	Cooking	Total Time
15 m	1 h 15 m	1 h 30 m

Nutritional Information:

Calories	266 kcal
Fat	10.9 g
Carbohydrates	32.5g
Protein	12.4 g
Cholesterol	0 mg
Sodium	17 mg

* Percent Daily Values are based on a 2,000 calorie diet.

Mexican Style Kale

Ingredients
- 2 tbsps olive oil
- 1 C. shredded carrot
- 1 C. diced onion
- 5 cloves garlic, minced
- 6 C. vegetable broth
- 1 (16 oz.) package dry lentils
- 1 (24 oz.) jar chunky-style salsa
- 1 pinch cayenne pepper, or to taste
- salt and ground black pepper to taste
- 1 bunch kale, diced

Directions
- Stir fry your minced garlic, onions, and carrots in olive oil for 9 mins then add in the broth, salsa, and lentils.
- Get the mix boiling then place a lid on the pan and cook the contents for 50 mins with a low heat.
- Add in the pepper, salt, cayenne and kale and cook everything for 7 more mins.
- Enjoy.

Amount per serving (6 total)

Timing Information:

Preparation	Cooking	Total Time
15 m	55 m	1 h 10 m

Nutritional Information:

Calories	377 kcal
Fat	6.5 g
Carbohydrates	62.2g
Protein	22.7 g
Cholesterol	0 mg
Sodium	1182 mg

* Percent Daily Values are based on a 2,000 calorie diet.

LEMON AND KALE WITH GARLIC AND LENTILS

Ingredients
- 2 tbsps olive oil
- 1 onion, diced
- 1 carrot, diced
- 3 cloves garlic, minced
- 4 thyme sprigs
- 1/2 tsp kosher salt
- ground black pepper to taste
- 1/2 tsp crushed red pepper flakes, or to taste
- 1/2 pound green lentils
- 1 (14.5 oz.) can diced tomatoes, undrained
- 3 C. chicken broth
- 1 bunch dinosaur kale, stems removed and leaves roughly diced
- 1 lemon, zested and juiced

Directions
- Stir fry your carrots and onions in olive oil for 6 mins then add in: pepper flakes, garlic, black pepper, thyme sprigs, and kosher salt.
- Stir fry everything for 2 more mins then add: stock, tomatoes and liquid, and the lentils.
- Place a lid on the pot and cook the mix for 42 mins with a gentle boil.
- Pour in your lemon juice, zest, and the kale.
- Now cook the kale for 7 more mins then add some pepper and salt.
- Enjoy.

Amount per serving (4 total)

Timing Information:

Preparation	Cooking	Total Time
10 m	50 m	1 h

Nutritional Information:

Calories	368 kcal
Fat	8.8 g
Carbohydrates	55.4g
Protein	20.6 g
Cholesterol	4 mg
Sodium	1169 mg

* Percent Daily Values are based on a 2,000 calorie diet.

Honey and Ginger Lentils

Ingredients
- 1 pound dry lentils
- 1 small bay leaf
- 2 C. water
- 2 (14.5 oz.) cans chicken broth
- 2 tsps salt
- 1 tsp dry mustard
- 1/4 tsp ground ginger
- 1 tbsp soy sauce
- 1/2 C. diced onion
- 1 C. water
- 1/2 C. honey

Directions
- Get the following boiling in a saucepan: salt, lentils, broth, bay leaf, and 2 C. of water.
- Place a lid on the pan, set the heat to low, and cook everything for 35 mins. The bay leaf can be thrown away at this point.
- Set your oven to 350 degrees before doing anything else.
- Get a bowl, combine: 1 C. water, dry mustard, onions, soy sauce, and ginger.
- Combine this mustard mix with the lentils and top everything with the honey.
- Stir the contents well and place the lid back on the lentils.
- Put everything in the oven for 65 mins then stir the contents.
- Enjoy.

Amount per serving (8 total)

Timing Information:

Preparation	Cooking	Total Time
10 m	1 h 30 m	1 h 40 m

Nutritional Information:

Calories	234 kcal
Fat	0.7 g
Carbohydrates	46.4g
Protein	13.2 g
Cholesterol	0 mg
Sodium	1036 mg

* Percent Daily Values are based on a 2,000 calorie diet.

LENTILS FROM COLOMBIA

Ingredients
- 1/2 C. lentils
- 1 1/2 C. water
- 1 small tomato, diced
- 1 small onion, diced
- 2 tsps ground cumin
- 1 tsp salt
- 1 tbsp vegetable oil
- 2 small yellow potatoes, cubed

Directions
- Get the following boiling: veggie oil, lentils, salt, water, cumin, tomato, and onions. Get all the contents boiling for 35 mins then combine in the potatoes and cook the mix for 17 more mins.
- Enjoy.

Amount per serving (3 total)

Timing Information:

Preparation	Cooking	Total Time
10 m	45 m	55 m

Nutritional Information:

Calories	201 kcal
Fat	5.3 g
Carbohydrates	31.1g
Protein	9.3 g
Cholesterol	0 mg
Sodium	789 mg

* Percent Daily Values are based on a 2,000 calorie diet.

LENTILS FROM ARMENIA

Ingredients
- 2 tbsps olive oil
- 1 yellow onion, diced
- 4 C. water
- 1 C. lentils
- 1/4 C. bulgur
- 1 tsp salt
- 1 tsp ground black pepper
- 1 lemon, quartered
- 2 green onions, diced
- 1 C. plain yogurt

Directions
- For 9 mins stir fry your onions in oil then remove them from the pan.
- Get your lentils boiling in water then set the heat to a low level and cook the lentils for 17 mins.
- Add in the pepper, salt, and bulgur and cook them for 12 more mins before mixing in the onions.
- Now shut the heat, place a lid on the pot, and let the contents stand for 7 mins.
- Separate your lentils into four bowls, then place a garnishing of yogurt, green onions, and a lime wedge over each.
- Enjoy.

Amount per serving (4 total)

Timing Information:

Preparation	Cooking	Total Time
10 m	35 m	48 m

Nutritional Information:

Calories	285 kcal
Fat	8.4 g
Carbohydrates	40.6g
Protein	16 g
Cholesterol	4 mg
Sodium	922 mg

* Percent Daily Values are based on a 2,000 calorie diet.

LENTILS FROM PERSIA

Ingredients
- 1 pound uncooked white rice, soaked in water for 4 hrs
- 4 C. water, or as needed
- 1/2 tsp salt
- 2 C. water, or more as needed
- salt to taste
- 2 C. dry lentils, rinsed
- 1/4 C. vegetable oil, divided
- 2 large onions, thinly sliced
- 1/2 tsp saffron
- 1/3 C. hot water
- 3/4 C. pitted, diced dates
- 3/4 C. raisins

Directions
- Get a bowl, combine: 1/3 C. of hot water and the saffron.
- Let this stand.
- Get the following boiling: 4 C. fresh water, soaked rice, and half tsp salt.
- Now place a lid on the pot, set the heat to low, and let the rice cook for 13 mins.
- Then remove any excess liquids from the pan.
- Get another 2 C. of water, salt, and your lentils boiling and cook the mix with a gentle boil for 17 mins. Then shut the heat.

- Begin to stir fry your onions in 2 tbsps of veggie oil for 22 mins then remove them from the pan.
- Grab another saucepan and get 2 tbsps of veggie oil hot before adding in half of your rice.
- Now add the lentils and the rest of the rice.
- Place a lid on the pot, set the heat to a low level, and cook the mix for 22 mins.
- Now add in the water and saffron.
- Place the lid back on the pot and cook the contents for 12 more mins.
- Now begin to fluff your rice while stirring and breaking the hard bits at the bottom. Garnish your servings with fried onions, raisins, and dates.
- Enjoy.

NOTE: The hard bits of rice at the bottom of the pan are intended. And should be enjoyed by breaking it up and evenly mixing it throughout the rice before serving it!

Amount per serving (8 total)

Timing Information:

Preparation	Cooking	Total Time
20 m	1 h 15 m	4 h 35 m

Nutritional Information:

Calories	537 kcal
Fat	7.9 g
Carbohydrates	100.4g
Protein	17.7 g
Cholesterol	0 mg
Sodium	209 mg

* Percent Daily Values are based on a 2,000 calorie diet.

BROWN SUGAR, KALE, AND ONION LENTILS

Ingredients
- 1 C. olive oil
- 1 large red onion
- 1 (8 oz.) package dry lentils, rinsed and sorted
- water to cover
- 1 (6 oz.) can tomato paste
- 3 cloves garlic, diced
- 1 tbsp brown sugar
- 1 tbsp paprika
- 1 bunch kale, or to taste, diced
- salt to taste
- freshly ground black pepper to taste

Directions
- Stir fry your red onions in olive oil for 9 mins then add in the lentils and submerge everything in water with an additional 2 inches.
- Get the mix boiling then set the heat to a low level.
- Add in the paprika, tomato paste, brown sugar, and garlic.
- Let the contents gently boil for 65 mins over low heat.
- Add the kale and continue cooking for 13 more mins then add in pepper and salt.
- Enjoy.

Amount per serving (12 total)

Timing Information:

Preparation	Cooking	Total Time
15 m	1 h 20 m	1 h 35 m

Nutritional Information:

Calories	267 kcal
Fat	18.6 g
Carbohydrates	20.5g
Protein	6.9 g
Cholesterol	0 mg
Sodium	132 mg

* Percent Daily Values are based on a 2,000 calorie diet.

LENTILS FROM INDIA II

Ingredients
- 1/4 C. cooking oil
- 12 cashews
- 2 dried red chile peppers
- 1 tsp cumin seed
- 1 tsp mustard seed
- 10 black peppercorns
- 1 pinch asafoetida powder
- 1 C. split yellow lentils (moong dal)
- 1 C. rice
- 1/2 C. shredded coconut
- 2 green chile peppers, diced
- 1/2 tsp ground turmeric
- salt to taste
- 3 1/2 C. water
- 2 tbsps ghee
- 1/4 C. diced cilantro leaves
- 1/4 C. shredded coconut

Directions
- Pour your oil into a pressure cooker and get it hot. Then begin to fry the nuts in the oil.
- When cashews are browned remove them from the pressure cooker.
- Add in: asafoetida, red chili peppers, peppercorns, cumin seeds, and the mustard seeds.
- Let these spices cook for 4 mins before adding in the lentils and cooking the mix for 3 more mins.
- Now combine in: water, rice, turmeric, salt, 1/2 C. coconut, and chili peppers.
- Set your pressure cooker for 15 pounds of pressure, with the lid closed tightly, and cook the rice for 37 mins.

- Open the cooker after safely letting out the pressure and combine in the ghee and cashews.
- When serving your rice and lentils top everything with some cilantro and 1/4 C. of coconut.
- Enjoy.

Amount per serving (6 total)

Timing Information:

Preparation	Cooking	Total Time
10 m	40 m	50 m

Nutritional Information:

Calories	419 kcal
Fat	18.2 g
Carbohydrates	52.9g
Protein	12 g
Cholesterol	11 mg
Sodium	121 mg

* Percent Daily Values are based on a 2,000 calorie diet.

Kootu

(Lentils from South India)

Ingredients
- 1/2 C. red lentils
- 1/2 C. hulled, split pigeon peas (toor dal)
- 1/2 C. yellow split peas
- 2 C. water
- 2 tbsps vegetable oil
- 1 tsp mustard seed
- 4 leaves fresh curry leaves
- 1 carrot, peeled and diced
- 1 zucchini, sliced
- 1/4 C. frozen peas
- 1/4 tsp ground turmeric
- 1 tbsp crushed red pepper flakes
- salt to taste
- 1/4 C. grated fresh coconut

Directions
- Get the following boiling: water, red lentils, slit peas, and pigeon peas.
- Place a lid on the pot, set the heat to low, and let the contents gently cook for 35 mins.

- At the same time stir fry your mustard seeds in veggie oil for 3 mins then add the carrots and curry leaves.
- Cook the mix for 6 more mins before adding in the salt, zucchini, pepper flakes, peas, and turmeric.
- Stir fry this mix for 7 mins then add the coconut, and cooked peas.
- Enjoy.

Amount per serving (4 total)

Timing Information:

Preparation	Cooking	Total Time
25 m	30 m	55 m

Nutritional Information:

Calories	315 kcal
Fat	9.9 g
Carbohydrates	42.5g
Protein	16.2 g
Cholesterol	0 mg
Sodium	129 mg

* Percent Daily Values are based on a 2,000 calorie diet.

LENTILS FROM INDIA III

Ingredients

- 1 C. lentils
- 1/4 C. dry kidney beans (optional)
- water to cover
- 5 C. water
- 2 tbsps salt
- 2 tbsps vegetable oil
- 1 tbsp cumin seeds
- 4 cardamom pods
- 1 cinnamon stick, broken
- 4 bay leaves
- 6 whole cloves
- 1 1/2 tbsps ginger paste
- 1 1/2 tbsps garlic paste
- 1/2 tsp ground turmeric
- 1 pinch cayenne pepper, or more to taste
- 1 C. canned tomato puree, or more to taste
- 1 tbsp chili powder
- 2 tbsps ground coriander
- 1/4 C. butter
- 2 tbsps dried fenugreek leaves (optional)
- 1/2 C. cream (optional)

Directions

- Let your kidney beans and lentils sit submerged in water for 8 hrs.
- Then simmer them in 5 C. of fresh water, in a saucepan, for 65 mins.
- Reserve any liquids remaining in the pan.
- Now for 3 mins toast your cumin seeds in veggie oil then add in the cloves, a cinnamon stick, and the cardamom.
- Toast the seasonings for 2 mins then set the heat to low and combine in: cayenne, turmeric, garlic and ginger paste.

- Stir the contents for 15 secs then add in the tomato puree and cook the mix for 6 mins.
- Now add: butter, chili powder, and coriander.
- Once the butter is melted add the beans, lentils, and any reserved lentil liquids.
- Get everything boiling, set the heat to low, and let the contents cook for 50 mins with a lid on the pot.
- After 50 mins of cooking add your cream and heat it for 3 more mins.
- Stir the mix and serve.
- Enjoy.

Amount per serving (6 total)

Timing Information:

Preparation	Cooking	Total Time
15 m	2 h	4 h 15 m

Nutritional Information:

Calories	375 kcal
Fat	21.2 g
Carbohydrates	34.2g
Protein	12.8 g
Cholesterol	48 mg
Sodium	2718 mg

* Percent Daily Values are based on a 2,000 calorie diet.

LENTILS FROM LEBANON

Ingredients
- 6 C. chicken stock
- 1 pound red lentils
- 3 tbsps olive oil
- 1 tbsp minced garlic
- 1 large onion, diced
- 1 tbsp ground cumin
- 1/2 tsp cayenne pepper
- 1/2 C. diced cilantro
- 3/4 C. fresh lemon juice

Directions
- Get your lentils boiling in vegetable stock, then place a lid on the pan, set the heat to low, and let the contents gently cook for 22 mins.
- At the same time, stir fry your onions and garlic in olive oil for 5 mins then combine them with the lentils before adding in the cayenne and cumin.
- Cook this mix for 12 more mins then use an immersion blender to puree the mix.
- Finally add in the lemon juice and the cilantro.
- Enjoy.

Amount per serving (8 total)

Timing Information:

Preparation	Cooking	Total Time
20 m	30 m	50 m

Nutritional Information:

Calories	276 kcal
Fat	7 g
Carbohydrates	39.1g
Protein	16.7 g
Cholesterol	< 1 mg
Sodium	< 524 mg

* Percent Daily Values are based on a 2,000 calorie diet.

A Quiche of Lentils and Cheese

Ingredients
- 1 C. diced onion
- 2 tbsps olive oil
- 1/2 C. dried lentils
- 2 C. water
- 2 C. broccoli florets
- 1 C. diced fresh tomatoes
- 4 eggs, beaten
- 1 C. milk
- 1 tsp salt
- ground black pepper to taste
- 2 tsps Italian seasoning
- 1/2 C. shredded Cheddar cheese (optional)

Directions
- Set your oven to 375 degrees before doing anything else.
- Combine some olive oil and onions in a pie plate and cook the mix in the oven for 17 mins.
- At the same time get your lentils boiling in water and then cook them for 22 mins.
- Now remove any leftover liquids.
- Add the broccoli to the same pot as the lentils and place a lid over everything.
- Cook this mix for 7 mins.

- Combine the lentil mix and the tomatoes with the onions in the pie dish and then add the cheese as well.
- Get a bowl, combine: Italian seasoning, eggs, pepper, salt, and milk.
- Combine this mix with the lentils in the pie dish and cook everything in the oven for 50 mins.
- Enjoy.

Amount per serving (8 total)

Timing Information:

Preparation	Cooking	Total Time
15 m	1 h 15 m	1 h 30 m

Nutritional Information:

Calories	165 kcal
Fat	9.1 g
Carbohydrates	12.4g
Protein	9.7 g
Cholesterol	103 mg
Sodium	392 mg

* Percent Daily Values are based on a 2,000 calorie diet.

2 Bean Lentils

Ingredients
- 2 tbsps olive oil
- 1 large white onion, diced
- 1/2 C. dry lentils
- 2 cloves garlic, minced
- 3 tbsps curry powder
- 1 tsp ground cumin
- 1 pinch cayenne pepper
- 1 (28 oz.) can crushed tomatoes
- 1 (15 oz.) can garbanzo beans, drained and rinsed
- 1 (8 oz.) can kidney beans, drained and rinsed
- 1/2 C. raisins
- salt and pepper to taste

Directions
- Stir fry our onions in oil then add the cayenne, curry, cumin, pepper, salt, and lentils.
- Stir and heat this mix for 3 mins then add the: raisins, tomatoes, kidney beans, and garbanzos.
- Set the heat to a low level and cook the mix for 65 mins with a gentle simmer.
- Enjoy.

Amount per serving (8 total)

Timing Information:

Preparation	Cooking	Total Time
15 m	1 h 10 m	1 h 25 m

Nutritional Information:

Calories	208 kcal
Fat	4.7 g
Carbohydrates	35.9g
Protein	8.7 g
Cholesterol	0 mg
Sodium	298 mg

* Percent Daily Values are based on a 2,000 calorie diet.

UPSTATE NEW YORK LENTILS

Ingredients
- 2 tbsps butter
- 1 onion, diced
- 2/3 C. red lentils
- 1/2 C. orange juice
- 1 stalk celery, diced
- 1/2 carrot, shredded
- 1 bay leaf
- 1/2 tsp dried thyme
- ground black pepper to taste
- 3 C. chicken broth, divided

Directions
- Stir fry your onions in butter then add in: half of the broth, lentils, pepper, orange juice, thyme, celery, bay leaf, and carrots.
- Let the contents gently boil for 45 mins then grab your immersion blender and puree the contents into a soup.
- Add the rest of the broth and get everything hot again.
- Enjoy.

Amount per serving (4 total)

Timing Information:

Preparation	Cooking	Total Time
15 m	1 h	1 h 15 m

Nutritional Information:

Calories	172 kcal
Fat	6.2 g
Carbohydrates	22.6g
Protein	7.9 g
Cholesterol	15 mg
Sodium	242 mg

* Percent Daily Values are based on a 2,000 calorie diet.

Lentils from Morocco II

Ingredients
- 1/2 C. dry lentils
- 1 1/2 C. water
- 1/2 (15 oz.) can garbanzo beans, drained
- 2 tomatoes, diced
- 4 green onions, diced
- 2 minced hot green chili peppers
- 1 green bell pepper, diced
- 1/2 yellow bell pepper, diced
- 1 red bell pepper, diced
- 1 lime, juiced
- 2 tbsps olive oil
- 1/4 C. diced fresh cilantro
- salt to taste

Directions
- Get your water and lentils boiling then set the heat to low and gently cook the lentils for 35 mins.
- Get a bowl, mix: salt, lentils, cilantro, chickpeas, olive oil, tomatoes, lime juice, green onions, bell pepper, and green chilies.
- Place a covering of plastic around the bowl and put everything in the fridge for 25 mins.
- Enjoy.

Amount per serving (5 total)

Timing Information:

Preparation	Cooking	Total Time
10 m	1 h	1 h 10 m

Nutritional Information:

Calories	190 kcal
Fat	6.3 g
Carbohydrates	27.6g
Protein	8.1 g
Cholesterol	0 mg
Sodium	94 mg

* Percent Daily Values are based on a 2,000 calorie diet.

SWEET TOMATO LENTILS

Ingredients

- 3 C. water
- 1 C. lentils, rinsed
- salt to taste (optional)
- 1 C. diced onion
- 3 tbsps olive oil
- 2 C. diced tomato
- 2 cloves garlic, minced
- 1/2 (6 oz.) can tomato paste
- 1/2 C. ketchup
- 1 tsp mustard powder
- 1 tbsp chili powder
- 3 tbsps molasses
- 1 dash Worcestershire sauce
- salt and ground black pepper to taste
- 4 hamburger buns, split

Directions

- Get your lentils boiling in water and salt, then set the heat to low and cook them for 35 mins.
- At the same time stir fry your onions in olive oil for 6 mins then add in the garlic and tomatoes.
- Cook the tomatoes for 6 mins then add: Worcestershire, tomato paste, molasses, ketchup, chili powder, and mustard powder.
- Let this mix cook for 7 mins until it is thick.
- Now remove any liquids from the lentils and save it.
- Combine the lentils with the tomatoes mix then add in the reserved lentil liquid.
- Stir the contents and try to form a wet but thick mix.
- Enjoy on toasted sesame seed buns.

NOTE: These sweet tomato style lentils are a replacement for the American "Sloppy Joes" which is a similar dish but prepared with ground beef and enjoyed for lunch oftentimes.

Amount per serving (4 total)

Timing Information:

Preparation	Cooking	Total Time
15 m	35 m	50 m

Nutritional Information:

Calories	517 kcal
Fat	13.9 g
Carbohydrates	82.2g
Protein	19.3 g
Cholesterol	0 mg
Sodium	782 mg

* Percent Daily Values are based on a 2,000 calorie diet.

CHILI I

Ingredients
- 2 tbsps vegetable oil
- 1 onion, diced
- 4 cloves garlic, minced
- 1 C. dry lentils
- 1 C. dry bulgur wheat
- 3 C. low fat, low sodium chicken broth
- 2 C. canned whole tomatoes, diced
- 2 tbsps chili powder
- 1 tbsp ground cumin
- salt and pepper to taste

Directions
- Stir fry your garlic and onions in oil for 7 mins then add the bulgur, pepper, broth, salt, tomatoes, cumin, chili powder, and lentils.
- Get everything boiling, set the heat to low, and let the contents cook for 35 mins.
- Enjoy.

Amount per serving (6 total)

Timing Information:

Preparation	Cooking	Total Time
10 m	40 m	50 m

Nutritional Information:

Calories	281 kcal
Fat	6.1 g
Carbohydrates	45g
Protein	13.8 g
Cholesterol	0 mg
Sodium	376 mg

* Percent Daily Values are based on a 2,000 calorie diet.

LENTILS FROM THE MEDITERRANEAN II

Ingredients
- 1 1/4 C. orzo pasta
- 6 tbsps olive oil, divided
- 3/4 C. dried brown lentils, rinsed and drained
- 1/3 C. red wine vinegar
- 3 cloves garlic, minced
- 1/2 C. kalamata olives, pitted and diced
- 1 1/2 C. crumbled feta cheese
- 1 small red onion, diced
- 1/2 C. finely diced fresh mint leaves
- 1/2 C. diced fresh dill
- salt and pepper to taste

Directions
- Boil your pasta in water and salt for 9 mins then remove all the liquids and add the pasta to a bowl with a tbsp of olive oil.
- Place a covering on the bowl and chill everything in the fridge.
- Not get your lentils boiling in water, then place a lid on the pot, and let them cook with a low level of heat for 22 mins.
- Remove any excess liquids and let them cool off.
- Get a 2nd bowl, combine: garlic, olive oil, and vinegar.
- Now combine your lentils with the pasta and add: the vinegar mix, dill, olive, mint, red onions, and feta.

- Add some pepper and salt then place everything in the fridge for 60 more mins to get cold.
- Enjoy.

Amount per serving (8 total)

Timing Information:

Preparation	Cooking	Total Time
30 m	20 m	2 h 50 m

Nutritional Information:

Calories	374 kcal
Fat	19 g
Carbohydrates	38.2g
Protein	13.3 g
Cholesterol	25 mg
Sodium	456 mg

* Percent Daily Values are based on a 2,000 calorie diet.

Lentil Burgers

(Vegetarian Approved)

Ingredients
- 1 C. dry brown lentils
- 2 1/2 C. water
- 1/4 C. milk
- 1 C. wheat and barley nugget cereal (e.g. Grape-Nuts(TM))
- 1 (1 oz.) envelope dry onion soup mix
- 1/2 tsp poultry seasoning
- 2 eggs, beaten
- 1/2 C. diced walnuts
- 1 C. seasoned dry bread crumbs
- 2 tbsps vegetable oil

Directions
- Get your lentils boiling in water then place a lid on the pot, and set the heat to low.
- Let the lentils cook for 35 mins then remove any resulting liquids.
- Get a bowl, combine: walnuts, poultry spice, lentils, soup mix, eggs, milk, wheat and barley.
- Use your hands to knead the mix then let it rest for 40 mins.
- Now fry patties of this mix in hot oil after you've coated them with bread crumbs.

- Cook each patty for 6 mins then flip it and fry for 6 more mins.
- Enjoy.

Amount per serving (8 total)

Timing Information:

Preparation	Cooking	Total Time
30 m	30 m	1 h

Nutritional Information:

Calories	289 kcal
Fat	11.1 g
Carbohydrates	37.8g
Protein	12.3 g
Cholesterol	47 mg
Sodium	683 mg

* Percent Daily Values are based on a 2,000 calorie diet.

LENTILS FROM MOROCCO III

Ingredients
- 6 C. beef stock
- 1 C. dry lentils
- 1 tbsp olive oil, or to taste
- 1 onion, diced
- 1 cinnamon stick
- 1 tsp minced fresh ginger root
- 1 tsp ground turmeric
- 1 tsp ground cumin
- 1 tsp ground black pepper
- 1 (15 oz.) can garbanzo beans, drained
- 1 (15 oz.) can red kidney beans, rinsed and drained
- 1 (14 oz.) can diced tomatoes
- 1 C. cooked quinoa (optional)
- 1 bunch flat-leaf parsley leaves and thinner stems, diced
- 1 bunch cilantro leaves and thinner stems, diced
- 1 lemon, or to taste, juiced

Directions
- Get your lentils boiling in beef stock.
- Now set the heat to a low level and let it gently cook while you stir fry your onions in olive oil for 2 mins.
- Add to the onions: black pepper, cinnamon stick, cumin, ginger, and turmeric.
- Cook the seasoned onions for 4 more mins then add them to the lentils and stir everything.
- Now combine the following with the lentils: quinoa, garbanzos, tomatoes, and kidney beans.
- Get everything boiling again and add the cilantro and parsley.
- Set the heat to its lowest level and gently cook the mix for 50 mins.

- Top the soup with some lemon juice then serve.
- Enjoy.

Amount per serving (10 total)

Timing Information:

Preparation	Cooking	Total Time
15 m	1 h	1 h 15 m

Nutritional Information:

Calories	261 kcal
Fat	3.9 g
Carbohydrates	42g
Protein	14.4 g
Cholesterol	0 mg
Sodium	299 mg

* Percent Daily Values are based on a 2,000 calorie diet.

CREAMY CLARIFIED LENTILS

Ingredients
- 3/4 C. dry brown lentils, soaked in water for 8 hrs
- 1/4 C. dry red lentils
- 4 C. water
- 5 whole garlic cloves
- 3/4 tsp salt
- 1/2 tsp ground coriander
- 1/2 tsp cayenne pepper, or to taste
- 1/4 tsp ground turmeric
- 2 tbsps clarified butter
- 1/4 onion, sliced
- 1 tsp ground cumin
- 1/8 C. milk (optional)
- 1 tbsp minced fresh cilantro

Directions
- Get the following boiling in a saucepan: turmeric, water, cayenne, garlic, coriander, salt, and lentils.
- Place a lid on the pot and let the lentils cook for 35 mins over a lower level of heat.
- Stir fry your onions in butter, while stirring, until they are brown, then add the cumin and fry everything for an additional min.
- Now combine the onions with the lentils and add the milk.
- Heat the contents for 7 more mins then top the mix with some cilantro.
- Enjoy.

Amount per serving (2 total)

Timing Information:

Preparation	Cooking	Total Time
15 m	40 m	1 h 55 m

Nutritional Information:

Calories	481 kcal
Fat	14.8 g
Carbohydrates	62.4g
Protein	26.3 g
Cholesterol	34 mg
Sodium	890 mg

* Percent Daily Values are based on a 2,000 calorie diet.

THANKS FOR READING! JOIN THE CLUB AND KEEP ON COOKING WITH 6 MORE COOKBOOKS....

http://bit.ly/1TdrStv

 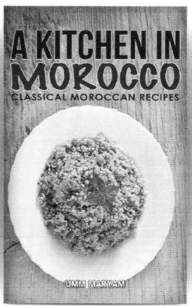 

To grab the box sets simply follow the link mentioned above, or tap one of book covers.

This will take you to a page where you can simply enter your email address and a PDF version of the box sets will be emailed to you.

Hope you are ready for some serious cooking!

http://bit.ly/1TdrStv

Come On...
Let's Be Friends :)

We adore our readers and love connecting with them socially.

Like BookSumo on Facebook and let's get social!

Facebook

And also check out the BookSumo Cooking Blog.

Food Lover Blog

36312235R00079

Printed in Great Britain
by Amazon